I0421960

TABLE OF CONTENTS

WARNING

The survival techniques and medical advice contained within this book are for extreme survival circumstances. Any misuse of advice that results in damage, loss or bodily harm is not the responsibility of the publisher or author. Please use common sense and seek a medical professional whenever possible. When practicing survival techniques, observe all laws protecting any particular species of plant in your region.

INTRODUCTION

Prepping is the most important thing you can do for your family in today's world. The weather is getting more dangerous every year with bigger hurricanes, monsoons, tornadoes and earthquakes happening everywhere. The possibility of a nuclear disaster as a result of any natural weather event is a real and present danger. With the worldwide economy being as unstable as it is, it is only smart to be prepared for the worst-case scenario.

There are lots of different ways to prep, as well as many different prepping goals. While most people are only prepared for one or two days after a disaster, there are those of us who are more concerned with surviving for weeks or months without the comforts of life as we know it in our climate controlled homes with running water. Anyone who is ever survived and that your disaster can tell you that there's a lot more to surviving then having enough cans of food or gallons of water. In a real disaster, help will not come soon enough. You may be weeks to months without water and will have to find a way to filter what you can find, or gather rainwater for everything from drinking to cooking.

There were also come a point where you would rather try to eat the tin can that the potted meat comes in then eat another bit of potted meat. Worst of all is the possibility of there not being anything to eat at all. Not only do you not want to be the person who doesn't have food, but you also need to be wary of others who might be in the situation where they do not have food. You have to be able to protect your family and the supplies that you have stored to secure their survival.

Of course, all of the supplies and tactics are only part of the survival puzzle. Anyone can survive for the first few days after disaster when they're adrenaline is going. A huge part of surviving is being able to keep a strong frame of mind. You can only be at full alert for so long before you become physically and mentally exhausted. Depending on the weather, and type of life that you've lived before, you might find yourself it to be extremely irritable and quick to anger. This is especially the case if you have gone from a climate controlled environment to one that is highly humid, hot, or dangerously cold. Failing to prepare to protect yourself from insect bites will take a toll not only on your health, but also on your mood.

By taking the time before a disaster to put together the proper kits that will ensure not just survival, but also some semblance of comfort, you will put yourself and your family and a much better place both physically and mentally. This means that you will need to not only prepare kits for hunkering down in your home, but you at also have to be prepared bug out and be on the move and still have everything that you need. There are even survival kits that will fit and a breath mint, just in case you are away from your home or vehicle when a sudden disaster happens.

The information in this guidebook will not only help you assemble the best possible kits for emergency situations, but it will also give you information you need to thrive and replenish your food and water stores.

72-HOUR KIT: SURVIVE

SHORT-TERM DISASTERS

There are countless scenarios to take into consideration when thinking about disaster preparation. Short-Scale disasters come with their own set of problems, and it's important to be ready for them. Many people simply think that they'll be able to get by for a while when faced with a temporary emergency. But what happens when you run through what you normally stock at home and you're still unable to obtain new supplies? This is why having a 72-hour survival plan is so important.

I don't always look at a 72-hour kit as something that must be used right away. Depending on the situation, it can be the last resort that you turn to when there's nothing left. Of course, it should be assembled in a way that makes it immediately accessible in case your first resort IS your last resort. Your family should be able to use its contents to survive for at least three days when the worst happens.

The 72-hour survival kit is actually pretty simple to put together, but there's always a chance that you'll overlook one or two things that you'll need when it's too late. A list of suggestions has been compiled on the following pages to assist in putting together a temporary survival bag that won't let you down when you need it. The following list is not comprehensive. There is a very good chance that your family's unique situation will require additional items for comfort. That is why it is absolutely vital to get together and make a list that suits your family's needs before creating your own kit. Just remember to keep it as light as possible; you never know when a disaster scenario will require you to leave your home to seek better cover.

- **Poncho** (Make sure it has a hood)

  This will protect you from torrential rain and keep your hands free. Soaking wet clothes are not only heavy, they are a sure way to get sick.

- **Body Warmers**

  These are a no-brainer. Your body has enough stress to deal with – trying to keep from getting hypothermia should not be one of them.

- **Tube Tent & Sleeping Bag**

  Simple and easy to move, this modest shelter may end up being the only thing between yourself and the elements.

- **Survival Whistle**

  You should not rely on your vocal chords to carry across vast distances. If you are lost or need to get the attention of a search and rescue team, this whistle can save your life with zero effort.

- **Nylon Rope** (Between 50 – 100 feet)

  People take for granted how many caves exist just beneath the surface. If you happen to be somewhere when the ground caves in, you can use a nylon rope to climb to safety. You can also tie it to a bucket and gather water from steep riverbanks or wells.

- **Pen / Pencil & Blank Notebook**

While you may not be writing your memoir in the wilderness, you may need to pass messages or make notes regarding plants, rivers or draw rough maps.

- **FM / Emergency Band Radio**

It is imperative to know what is happening in the world around you. Whether your biggest threat is weather phenomenon or a societal breakdown, you want to make sure that you are prepared for what is coming or keep away from problem areas.

- **Batteries**

Not only should you have batteries, you should also consider a solar-powered charging kit.

- **Garbage Bags & Ties**

    Cleaning up wreckage, hauling food or burying human waste are just some of the things that these bags will come in handy for.

- **Small Bottle of Hand Sanitizer**

    This is good for more than just washing your hands. It is also great for cleaning skin abrasions when nothing else is available.

- **Pliers** (In case utilities must be turned off)

- **Duct Tape**

- **N95 Dust Mask**

- **Swiss Army Knife**

- **Leather-Palm Work Gloves**

  Moving just one branch without these can result in a palm full of splinters and lower your survival chances significantly.

- **Toilet Paper**

  Keep in airtight freezer bag. This is more than just a sanitation item; it can also serve as a first aid item.

- **Waterproof Matches**

- **Small Shovel**

  You may need this for digging holes for sanitation purposes.

- **Basic First Aid Kit**

- **Hand-Cranked Flashlight**

- **Disposable Lighter**

- **30-Hour Emergency Candles**

- **Glow Sticks**

  Make sure they last 12 hours or more before

  buying.

- **High-Calorie Food Bars**

- **Lightweight** (but sturdy!) **Backpack**

- **Water Boxes**

- **Basic Hygiene Kit**

- **Plastic Sheet**

- **Change of Clothing**

- **Sleeping Pad**

- **Flares**

- **Full Gas Can**

  Everyone gets gas the day before a natural disaster – get yours before one ever gets announced. You will need this for your vehicle or generator. If you have neither, you can use it to trade for food or batteries.

- **Legal Documents** (Marriage Certificate, Birth Certificates, Wills, Passports, etc.)

- **Cash**

  Carry about $100 in small bills and a roll of quarters. Even when the power is back on, card processors can take much longer to start working again.

- **Local Map**

- **Basic Entertainment**

  Keep it light: a book, deck of cards, crayons, etc.

You will never be able to predict what will happen in a given scenario. While this list is not a comprehensive one, it should provide more than enough suggestions to keep your family comfortable through a short-scale disaster. If you are able to remain in your home during such a time, the supplies needed could be a bit more basic. In that case, make sure that you have a good supply of clean drinking water, basic medicines, food bars, sanitary items, and whatever your family's needs might be for that period of time. Always keep a full gas can handy in case you are unable to get to a filling station.

In many scenarios, you will be required to take cover elsewhere. This is where the duct tape, plastic sheets, emergency toilet paper, and sleeping pads come in handy. A good sleeping pad and sleeping bag will keep you off the cold ground. The duct tape and plastic sheeting can be used to build a temporary shelter for protection against the elements. If you must travel on foot, keep all legal documents sealed in plastic (large freezer bags work well in this situation). You don't want them to get damaged in rain, sleet, snow or worse.

Always be sure to pack your survival items in a lightweight, but sturdy backpack. After all, if you're travelling, you don't want to be weighed down unnecessarily.

MULTI-PURPOSE 5-GALLON BUCKET KIT

Disaster preparation is more important now than ever before. With major natural disasters popping up in record numbers, not to mention the current state of the economy in

North America and abroad, the worst is inevitable. At this point, it is only a matter of time before we must all be ready to employ survival methods in order to keep our loved ones out of harm's way. There are many ways to begin to prepare for disasters of all shapes and sizes, but as always, it is important to start with the basics.

The idea of a compact survival kit is nothing new, but it absolutely is a vital step in preparation. One such method of creating this kit is to utilize a food-grade 5-gallon bucket. The 5-gallon bucket survival kit is an extremely effective way to get started. These kits have grown in popularity to the point that they can be purchased online and in select physical stores, already assembled and ready to go. Just be aware that if you do buy a pre-assembled 5-gallon bucket survival kit, it will not be personalized to suit the needs of you or your family. The best way is to make your own, and the good news is that it's a lot easier than you might think.

First, be sure that the 5-gallon buckets and lids you use are made of food-grade plastics. If you are unsure about this, ask a salesperson. They should be able to tell you if they sell them or not. If the store doesn't carry food-grade buckets, go elsewhere, unless you're only planning on storing general supplies. In that case, there are a variety of buckets that you can use for these kits. Collapsible buckets even exist for extreme portability. In the case of this chapter, we will from now on assume that you have a food-grade, plastic 5-gallon bucket and lid.

The following pages of this chapter mostly consist of lists of useful items that should be considered for your survival bucket. When putting together yours, it's important to note that every item listed will not fit into one container. It is up to you to choose which products are best for your unique situation. Some people choose to have more than one bucket, due to necessity. The best thing about using the 5-gallon bucket method is that it's portable and can be carried wherever you need to go without much difficulty. The bucket itself, when empty, can actually be used as a floatation device in extreme circumstances, as long as the lid is fastened tightly. The air trapped in the bucket will keep you afloat in deep water. Lastly, a simple set of shoulder straps can be created with enough duct tape if you are unable to carry the bucket by its handle for extended periods of time.

Now, before we get into the list of supplies, your bucket should be separated into the following THREE categories:

- General Supplies

- First Aid Supplies

- Hygiene Supplies

GENERAL SUPPLIES

The following list contains suggestions for general / everyday items that would fit well in any 5-gallon survival bucket. This is meant to provide you with an idea of which items are useful and why. Your kit can be personalized to suit the needs of your unique situation.

- Additional Batteries (You can never have too many in an emergency situation)

- Blank Notebooks / Journals / Pens / Pencils

- Glow Sticks (Get the longest-lasting possible. Typically, 12-hour sticks will do)

- Flashlights (I always suggest having more than one handy. Keep several, and be sure to test them on a monthly basis)

- Hand-Cranked Flashlights

- Hand-Cranked AM / FM / Emergency Band Radio

- Hand Warmers

- Small Tarps (These can come in handy in a variety of emergency situations)

- Duct Tape / Electrical Tape

- N95 Dust Respirators

- Durable Trash Bags

- Small Can Opener

- Sewing Kit (This serves far more purposes than simply mending clothing)

- Matchbooks (I also recommend getting some small boxes of wooden matches)

- Safety Goggles

- Durable Leather Gloves

- Liquid Candle

- Zip Ties

- Police Whistle

- Thermal (Mylar) Blankets

- Paracord

- Two-Way Radios

- Small Multi-Tool (You never know when tiny screwdrivers or a pocketknife might come in handy. A good multifunction tool will have several screwdrivers, a small knife or two, and perhaps a can opener. There are plenty of makes and models that suit different needs.)

- Twine / Rope

- Super Glue

  Not only for its adhesive properties, also its use as liquid bandage.

- Flint

- Fire-Starting Kit (This kit was covered earlier)

- Solar-Powered Yard Light

- Fishing Line / Fish Hooks

It's easy to understand why some of these items might seem unnecessary, or overkill at the very least. In reality, it is always better to have what is needed during a catastrophe than having to go without. Some of the uses of these items are as follows:

Depending on the situation, two-way radios are quite useful in situations that require keeping in contact with members of your party across short distances. When the power goes out, and you're no longer getting a cellphone signal, staying in contact with your party could be the difference between life and death. These radios are compact enough to keep in your 5-gallon bucket and should be tested once every month along with the flashlights and AM/FM radio.

Batteries are always useful in any emergency. Make sure that you check the expiration date on them to ensure that you're not stuck powering your important emergency gear with weak batteries. Discard and replace as necessary. Blank notebooks or journals are also indispensable. They allow you to keep track of your inventory, record important events, and so forth. Glow sticks can be used in situations where you need light for an extended amount of time. Using these will help keep the batteries in your flashlights fresh.

N95 dust respirators are a no-brainer in any emergency kit. They can be a little on the pricey side, but they're worth every penny. Finally, the multifunction tool is extremely portable and is good for countless uses. It takes virtually no space in your survival bucket. Finally, if you are very careful, rolls of duct tape can be unraveled and re-wrapped around the outside of the 5-gallon bucket to save space inside.

FIRST AID SUPPLIES

The following list contains suggestions for medical/first aid items that would fit well in any 5-gallon survival bucket. This is meant to provide you with an idea of what can be stored for later use. Your kit can be personalized to suit the needs of your unique situation.

- Moist Towelettes

- Latex Gloves

- Hand Sanitizer

- Ace Bandages

- Band-Aids / Butterfly Bandages / Triangular Bandages

- Gauze Pads & Rolls

- Waterproof Medical Tape

- Cotton Balls & Swabs

- Antiseptic Towelettes

- Burn Cream

- Tylenol / Ibuprofen / Aspirin

- Benadryl

- Imodium A-D

- Hydrocortisone Cream

- Throat Lozenges

- Triple Antibiotic Ointment

- Earplugs

- Small Scissors

- Tweezers

- Petroleum Jelly

- Digital Thermometer

- Instant Ice Packs

- Small Bottle Hydrogen Peroxide

- Small Bottle Rubbing Alcohol

- Small Bee Sting Kit

- Earplugs

- Nail Clipper

- Potassium Iodide (To protect the thyroid from radiation in a radiological emergency)

- Basic Guide on Administering First Aid

- Benzocaine Oral Gel

There are other medical supplies to consider, based on your unique situation. These are all invaluable during any emergency. It is of the utmost importance that you keep a record of medicines and their expiration dates. Replace any expired drugs as needed. While many expired medicines are harmless, some can become toxic soon after their expiry date. Never take a chance on expired medication. Simply replace it and discard as directed on the manufacturer's packaging.

HYGIENE SUPPLIES

The following list contains suggestions for personal hygiene items that will serve as great additions to your 5-gallon survival bucket. This is meant to provide you with an idea of what can be stored for later use. Your kit can be personalized to suit the needs of your unique situation.

- Tissue Paper / Kleenex

- Dental Floss

- Toothpaste

- Portable Toothbrushes

- Comb / Collapsible Hairbrush

- Toilet Paper / Moist Sanitary Wipes

- Bar Soap

- Baby Shampoo

- Unscented Hand Lotion

- Feminine Hygiene Products

- Sunblock

- Travel-Sized Mouthwash

- Small Battery-Powered Shaver

- Razor & Boxes of Razorblades

It is important to remember that even certain hygiene products have expiration dates. Be sure to keep a physical inventory of items and their expiration dates. Always replace things as needed. Good hygiene is a major contributing factor to good health. These items go hand-in-hand with your emergency medical supplies. Keeping your body clean will keep germs and the risk of illness at a minimum.

CANDY TIN SURVIVAL KIT

Much has been said about building a larger survival kit, but now is the time to discuss building much smaller kits. Being able to keep the elements that you need to survive contained within a small candy tin could be of significant help down the road when you must pick up and leave, but have no space to carry large buckets of items with you. For the kit I will discuss in this section, we will be using a rectangular mint tin. The amount of items that you can keep in such a small storage space might just be surprising to you. You can literally fit the items that you will need to survive in an emergency for 48 to 72 hours (Not counting food and water, of course) inside of one of these little containers if you choose the correct thing and understand how to pack it.

The following page will include a list of items that can be kept in your candy tin survival kit. As always, this is not a comprehensive list. The items that you choose to store inside of your tin could vary depending on your family's situation. The items on the following page are listed in the order that they should be packed into the tin for the best overall fit.

- **Signal Mirror** – This can help you get noticed by passing vehicles, including planes and boats if you become stranded. This sits on the bottom of your kit.

- **Bandages** – Pack an assortment. These should rest on the bottom of your candy tin, just on top of the mirror. Make sure to include a few butterfly closures just in case.

- **Travel Size Tylenol or Aspirin** – These typically come in small, flat packages and can lie on top of the mirror and bandages.

- **Safety Pins** – Pack four of these. They will be the next item to go in the kit. They should rest comfortably to either side of the tin, just on top of the bandages.

- **Fishing Hooks, Sinkers and Fishing Line** – These can fit in two ways. Either place them off to the opposite side of your safety pins, or you can tape them underneath the lid of your tin. Pack three hooks, three sinkers and enough fishing line to be useful for catching fish.

- **Needle & Thread** – These can both be lightly taped underneath the lid of your kit. This will allow you to patch clothing and tarps, or stitch a wound in a serious emergency situation.

- **Small Can Opener** – This should be the next item to go in your kit. It can be slipped just underneath the safety pins. It should be small and have a flat body, which can be used as a screwdriver and prying tool, as well as opening cans.

- **Duct Tape** – Tightly wrap between six to nine feet of tape and fit it into your survival kit.

- **Waterproof Matches and Striker** – This should be able to lay flat in your kit without taking up much room. Keep about 15 matches handy.

- **Small Pocketknife** – This will lie across the bottom of the survival kit. If you did not tape other items underneath the lid, that can also be a good spot for your knife. A good, compact pocketknife will act as a hammer, cutting tool and more. Make sure your knife has a locking back for added security.

- **Compact Rescue Whistle** – There should still be plenty of room in your candy tin for one of these. This whistle will allow people to hear you from more than one mile away. If you get one with a lanyard hole, you can keep it around your neck at all times, leaving additional space in your tin for something else.

- **Portable Compass** – If you become lost or stranded, there might not be passerby around to find you. In this case, you will need to find your own way. Your kit should be feeling a bit tight at this point, but a small enough compass will still fit, leaving room for one or two more items of importance.

- **Cotton Tinder** – Cotton is an extremely useful source of fuel for your matches. Without something to start a fire, your matches will be useless. Try to find cotton that has been treated with waterproof agents.

SURVIVING A RIOT

Rule 1: Stay Calm

Do not get swept up in the chaos or panic. Keeping cool is the only thing that will help you.

Rule 2: Stay Together

If you are with other people when the riot breaks out, hold hands and stay as close as possible. Do not split up. Check on one another throughout the time that you are stuck in the riot.

Rule 3: Avoid Weapons

This seems like a no-brainer, but avoid chemical weapons (mace, gas, smoke) and go in the opposite way of loud sounds that could be gunfire.

Rule 4: Find an Exit

If you are stuck indoors, look for a way out of the building.

Rule 5: Get Indoors

Most riots happen in halls or on streets. If getting outdoors is not possible (say you are on the second floor of a mall and the riot has taken over the stairs), get out of the core of the riot and into a small space or get out of the street into any building.

SURVIVING A FLOOD

Rule 1: Assess Damages Ahead of Time

Before a flood ever happens, you need to look at your home and the surrounding area and estimate what kind of damage you can expect. Know what points are the weakest and most dangerous. When a flood does occur, you will know which areas are the safest and which to avoid.

Rule 2: Be Aware

You cannot be prepared for a flood if you do not even know that it is going to rain. Pay close attention to local weather, as well as local weather patterns.

Rule 3: Collective Survival

Groups are more successful at surviving floods than individuals, so become involved in your community flood plan. If your community does not have one, make one yourself and share it. Do not underestimate the safety of numbers.

Rule 4: When to Bug Out

Grab your 72-Hour Kit and leave when the first flood warning is issued. Do not ever 'wait and see' how bad a flood can get. Get out of Dodge!

Rule 5: When to Hunker Down

If your home has already been hit by flood waters or a flood is expected within hours, stay put! You put yourself at much greater risk by going out into the water. Besides being trapped by flood water and being swept away by currents, there are other threats. While drowning is a very real concern, you can be pummeled by debris as large as a tool shed or mauled by frightened animals swept up by the current.

SURVIVING AN

EARTHQUAKE

Rule 1: Stay Informed

Even if your area is not on one of the active earthquake fault lines, find out if it is near an occasionally active one. You would be surprised to learn where earthquakes can happen.

Rule 2: Baby-Proof Your Home

Organize your home decor so that if an earthquake were to happen, you will get hit as little as possible by falling items.

- Install child-safe locks on cabinet doors

- Bolt shelves and tall furniture to wall studs

- Use screw-eyes to hang pictures, instead of nails

- Anchor down TVs and computers to surfaces with heavy-duty Velcro tape

- Keep breakables and heavy objects on bottom shelves

- Secure water heater to the wall by wrapping it with a strap and bolting it to wall studs

Rule 3: Find a Secure Place

Ride out the earthquake in the safest spot near where you are. That may be an open doorway, or it may be in an open field. Observe the safest places to be wherever you are and you will be prepared in the event of an earthquake. I once had an earthquake happen in the middle of an anniversary lunch, so never take your safety for granted.

SURVIVING A WILDFIRE

Rule 1: Be Ready to Run

Always have a 72-Hour Bug-Out Kit for each person, according to their needs. These kits should be within easy access. You should

NOT have to dig through a closet or push past several boxes in a tool shed to get to them.

Rule 2: Asses Your Home for Fire Hazards

Do you keep an extra gallon of gas in the tool shed? What about the gasoline in your lawn mower? Are there dead leaves in your gutters? Take a good look at all of the things in and around your home that could make you a prime target for a spreading fire. All it would take is a single cinder to land on your home for your family to be forced to run. Know your weaknesses and address them.

Rule 3: Build a Fire-Safe Wall

There are many different fire-resistant fences you can install around your home that would give your family a better chance of getting out of a fire's path in time. A line of hardwood trees are also a good choice. Do your research and find out what is or isn't allowed according to your HOA or zoning board.

Rule 4: Fire Alarms

This seems simple, but this failsafe often fails due to human error. Install them where you cook, where your heaters are installed and closest to where outdoor fires are the most likely to occur. Check the batteries often and do not just leave them turned off when you burn a meal and they start to annoy you. Get Carbon Monoxide alarms while you are at it, this silent killer is no less dangerous than flames.

Rule 5: Fire Extinguishers

Have one of these in every room of your home. The expense is worth it. No one ever plans which room they will be in when caught up in a fire, so keep more than just one in the kitchen. Small ones the size of aerosol cans are also available.

Rule 6: Share Fire Plans

Talk to your family about a safe place you can meet outside in the event of a fire. Discuss which windows to use, how to use an emergency fire ladder and unstick windows that might be painted shut. Always call the authorities if possible, but never risk your life to do so.

SURVIVING A HURRICANE

Rule 1: Be Prepared Beforehand

Get your supplies before the start of hurricane season. If you wait until a hurricane is announced to buy supplies, you may not find any left for sale or will be met with price gouging. Price gouging during an emergency may be illegal, but it still happens and you will not have time to argue the point when a storm is a day away.

Rule 2: Leave for Safety BEFORE the Storm

If you are staying at a shelter, be there before the winds pick up. If you are leaving town, be at your destination before the weather picks up. Being stuck in traffic with everyone else who waited until the last minute is a sure way to die.

Rule 3: Debunk the Taped Windows Myth

Taping your windows will not protect them or your home. Install shutters or board them up.

Rule 4: Store Water. Lots of Water.

Fill your bathtub with water. Depending on how bad the storm is, your life may depend on it later on.

Rule 5: Stay Inside During the Eye

If you are close enough to the center of the storm, you will cross right through the eye. It is very calm and quiet in the eye of a hurricane, but do NOT go outside to look. It is very dangerous outside due to the damage done by the first half of the storm, and the second half can fall on you full force at any moment.

Rule 5: Prepare for Post-Hurricane

Congratulations, you survived the hurricane. It may be days or months before the power is restored and proper water pressure is restored to your plumbing. Power cables are down everywhere, and flooding may be a serious problem. Be prepared to stay where you are and ration out your food. Splashing around in flood water contaminated with sewage waste is never a good idea.

SURVIVING A BIOLOGICAL

ATTACK

Rule 1: Do Not Count on Vaccines

While vaccines may become available,

you must have a contingency plan for protecting

yourself from infection and having enough supplies to isolate yourself in your home.

Rule 2: Stay Home

Do not send your children to school, go to work or go get last-minute supplies. Biological threats are too small to see with the naked eye and the only way to stay safe is to stay away. Many companies now offer work-from-home options. Call and talk to your employer about the possibility of working from home. Have at least 2 weeks' worth of food in your emergency pantry at all times.

Rule 3: Protect Your Face

Never touch your hands to your face and wash your hands frequently. Use an alcohol-based hand sanitizer. Wear eye protection, especially if you are forced to go into public. All it takes is one droplet from a sneeze to get infected.

Rule 4: Social Distancing

This may be the hardest, but sick people often do not look sick at first. Avoid social gatherings or meeting with other people until the threat has passed.

Rule 5: Wear a Respirator

These may be uncomfortable, but they will keep your precious lungs from inhaling any biological or chemical agents that can do you harm. They must be NIOSH certified and be N95, N99 or N100. They will only work if fitted properly, so make sure that you follow instructions when molding it to your face. You should not be able to smell perfume once you have it on and there should be no gaps.

Rule 6: Prepare for Utility Disruption

Be prepared to rough it without electricity or other utilities in the event that things get very bad. Hurricane preparedness kits are great for this type of emergency.

SURVIVING GUNFIRE

In the event of looting after a natural disaster or a government breakdown, people will do whatever is necessary when they are starving. This means that you may find yourself in the line of gunfire more than once. There are a few tips that you need to keep in mind that can help you get out of those situations alive.

If you are NOT the target:

Rule 1: Get down

Get flat on your stomach and stay calm. Stay as low as possible in relation to the shooter(s). Do not just crouch down.

Rule 2: Seek Protection

If you are near heavy furniture or a car, get to the side opposite the gunshots and lay low. If you are in the same room as a shooter, get to another room if possible and lay flat on your stomach. If you are face-to-face with the shooter, turn sideways immediately and hit the floor. Be less of a target by any means necessary.

Rule 3: Shooter Outside? Stay Inside.

If the shooter is outdoors, you do not want to go outdoors and be target that they can see. Stay indoors, away from windows and doors and lay flat on your stomach.

If YOU are the Target:

Rule 1: Run

Do not run in a straight line, be a difficult target and zigzag as much as possible and put as much distance between yourself and the shooter as you can.

Rule 2: Ruin the Shooter's Line-of-Sight

Turn a corner or duck behind buildings as soon as you can.

Rule 3: Don't Count Shots

Being in the line of gunfire is not like it is on TV or in the movies. Never assume that because the shots have paused that the shooter is out of bullets. You do not know how much ammo the shooter has, so keep running until you reach safety.

SHELTER: THE TREE PIT

If you find yourself knee-deep in snow in a forest and need to consider camping overnight, the tree pit can save your life.

Step 1: Walk to the nearest tree well.

A tree well is the area around the trunk of a tree that has accumulated less snow than the surrounding area.

Step 2: Dig.

Dig down to the bare ground and the perimeter around the tree that you need. Use anything you have at your disposal to help with the digging. Shoe shoes, frying pans, anything.

Step 3: Fortify.

Pack snow high around the perimeter to create a barrier between yourself and the wind. Tightly-packed snow will also help retain heat.

Step 4: Cover.

Cover your shelter with anything you may have at your disposal. Branches and other debris will work fine. Crawl in before putting the last bit of roofing on top.

SHELTER: THE PIT HOUSE

These longer-term shelters can be built just about anywhere and are as safe as you can get in a situation where your home is not safe, but you need to stay put for a while. They are also very simple to build.

Step 1: Location is Everything.

Find an elevated position that is not susceptible to flooding, such as the side of the hill.

Step 2: Dig.

Dig a huge hole. It is as simple as that. However much space you want in your pit shelter is as big as it needs to be.

Step 3: Reinforce.

You are going to want more than just mud and dirt for walls. Line and reinforce the walls with stripped logs, rocks or whatever materials you have available.

Step 4: Keep the Rain Out.

Put a roof on your pit. Use stripped logs, downed branches or whatever else you have available.

Step 5: Hide It.

You don't want to advertise to every passerby where your shelter is, so don't leave a giant pile of dirt nearby from where you dug. Spread it out and place some on top of your roof. Make it look natural – like it belongs there.

DETERMINING DANGEROUS PERSONS THROUGH BODY LANGUAGE

This information will serve you not only after a disaster or collapse, but also in your everyday life before a catastrophic event. Use this knowledge for everything from avoiding being mugged to turning people away from your encampment.

FACIAL CUES

- Pupil dilation: Very few people are able to control this.

- Pulse: Adrenalin will cause the pulse to quicken. It should be visible as a light visual thumping in the temples or neck.

- Perspiration: When nervous, most people are not able to control perspiration around their forehead.

- Mouth: An open mouth is a sign that the person isn't able to get enough oxygen for their increased heart rate just from their

nose.

UPPER BODY

Arms or hands above the waistline are always a threat. They can quickly withdraw a weapon or be used as weapons themselves. Arms from a nonthreatening person should be relaxed or at least below the waistline.

LOWER BODY

Legs in themselves are not dangerous, but they can be indicative of someone dangerous. If someone is concealing a weapon, they will subconsciously put their dominate foot in front of their other foot. If someone is standing on the balls of their feet, that is indicative that they are about to act.

MENTAL PREPAREDNESS

Survival in any situation only minimally dependent on your equipment. A clear and calm mind is the most important tool that you have. Prepare yourself for situations where you may lose your patience or panic. Expect to be overwhelmed and learn how to regain your composure.

Fear, anxiety, panic and depression will do more than affect your mood – it will also cause you to make bad decisions that can cost you and your family their lives. Train your mind to think positively in every situation. Never allow yourself to think that whatever situation you are in is going to be 'it' for you. Recognize your emotions, root out the cause and separate yourself from them. Think calmly and logically. Whether you need to disconnect yourself from the situation emotionally or take long breaths, keep control until the crisis is manageable.

Try these exercises:

- Do practice emergency drills every week with your family.

- Pick a mantra that works best for yourself when you are stressed. It might be 'stay calm,' 'focus,' or 'I got this.' Say it slowly and purposely to yourself when you need to focus.

- Breathe deeply (if it is safe to do so). Deeper breaths result in increased oxygenation to the blood.

- Pause between breaths and breathe through your nose.

WATER PURIFICATION

All seasoned preppers already understand that having clean water is paramount to survival. The amount of clean water needed per person, per day, is one gallon. Unfortunately, many scenarios could arise that require water to be purified before it is safe to drink. The bad news is that standard purification methods might not be available when we need them the most. Rest assured, there are alternative methods for creating clean drinking water for survival purposes. Whether you are accessing tap water that has been deemed undrinkable, or you get your supply from a local lake, there are three methods of purification that you can utilize.

Before we go any further, please note that you MUST be careful and use good judgment when dealing with iodine and other chemicals. These purification methods can be quite dangerous if used properly. Make sure you understand how these methods work inside and out before you actually do it.

Also keep in mind that should you seek out water through natural means (lakes, ponds, etc.), always choose a source of running water over stagnant. It will also benefit you a great deal to pay attention to the plants near the water source. Are the plants healthy? If you have any doubts, seek out another source of drinking water.

WATER PURIFICATION
METHODS

- Boiling

- Bleach Purification

- Iodine Purification

These three methods each come with a few notable pros and cons, but you will not find an easier way to create drinkable water in a disaster setting. Boiling water is the safest of the three, as it uses no chemicals in the process.

Iodine and bleach can be toxic if used incorrectly. Measurements should be followed exactly. If you do not feel comfortable working with chemicals, you should listen to your gut instinct and make sure that your survival kit includes the necessary tools for boiling water.

Furthermore, if after purification, the drinking water has a cloudy appearance, do not drink it, as there may still be toxins present from the original source. Gather more water and start over again from square one.

METHOD NO. 1: BOILING

As previously stated, this is the simplest and safest way to purify your gathered water in order to make it safe for drinking.

- Place gathered water into a pot or kettle

- Using whatever heat source is available to you, bring the water to a boil

- Continue at a rolling boil for at least 5 minutes

- Once the heat has been brought down and the water is at a comfortable temperature, it should be perfectly safe to drink. Any living bacteria should be dead.

This method will kill harmful bacteria that might be present in water that has been deemed undrinkable. Please note that if your water was obtained from a source that has been contaminated with harmful chemicals, boiling will not work. You should never attempt to purify or drink water that contains toxic agents!

METHOD NO. 2: BLEACH

Please use exact measurements and follow all directions carefully when working with bleach as a cleansing agent!

- Use 1/4 teaspoon of liquid, unscented household bleach per gallon of water.

- DO NOT drink the water until it has been sitting for at least an hour.

- DO NOT attempt to flavor the water with drink powders or syrups until it has been sitting for at least an hour.

This method works extremely well and has been in use for years. Since most households have at least a small supply of bleach on-hand, it's a simple and effective way to cleanse your water supply for drinking.

METHOD NO. 3: IODINE

Before attempting to use iodine to sterilize your water supply, make sure that you do not suffer from an iodine allergy. This would normally go without saying, but often, we don't know that we have a specific allergy until we come into contact with the culprit. This is why using iodine for water purification can be somewhat dangerous if you don't have a good understanding of your family history in regards to illness and allergies.

- Use Tincture of Iodine. This is available at most drug stores. It contains 47% alcohol and 2% iodine.)

- Add 8 drops to each liter of water.

- DO NOT drink the water until it sits for at least 20 minutes.

- DO NOT attempt to flavor the water with drink powders or syrups until it has been sitting for at least 20 minutes.

Again, if you think anyone in your family might have an allergy to iodine, use another purification method! Otherwise, this is a highly effective way to create drinkable water, although it will have a somewhat bitter taste.

GATHERING & STORING

WATER

Having a reliable and plentiful supply of drinking water is paramount to survival in any situation. That is precisely why methods to gather and store the water must be put in the place before you are faced with an emergency scenario. Drinkable water can be stored for quite some time if the conditions in which the supplies stored are sanitary, and if you bottle it correctly. Using clean containers will ensure that your water supply is free from contaminants, which means that you and your family will be able to use the supply for drinking, cleaning and more without having to worry about harmful bacteria.

Unfortunately, certain situations will ensure that you do not have access to an emergency supply of clean drinking water. In this case, you have to resort to other methods to capture in purify the water. Some of the purification methods, which will be mentioned later on, involve the years of chemicals. Other methods are safer and simpler if you have access to the right tools. Once you have learned to capture and purify your own drinking water from natural methods, you will be much better prepared any emergency situations where there are no laws, stores, or neighbors to fall back on.

The following pages will list several different methods for capturing your own drinking water, whether the sources come from rain, nearby lakes or other natural bodies of water. Make sure that you take the time to read each method and steps involved as carefully as possible before you attempt any of this. This knowledge is absolutely indispensable when you are stuck without a regular water source and need to hydrate yourself and your loved ones.

Whether you were dealing with world economic collapse, or you're simply lost in the woods, understanding how to survive in nature will help you significantly. The most important steps in that survival is making sure that you have uncontaminated water for hydration, cooking, and cleaning.

STORING WATER

Later sections will discuss how to purify water once you have captured, but for now, we will focus on the actual capturing. There are several ways to obtain drinking water when you do not have a supply of your own in the form of running water and your home. You can get water from lakes, rivers, and you can even obtain Rainwater that can be made safe for drinking in general use.

First, it is extremely important to understand how much water the average person needs for survival. A good rule of thumb is that the average person should have 1 gallon of drinkable water per day on hand. This does not include water that is used for bathing yourself or cooking food. If you are storing water in your home, be sure that all of your containers are BPA free and are capable of prohibiting light. This will ensure that algae do not grow the water, keeping your water safe and fresh for much longer. If using a water hose to fill your containers, make sure that it is a drink safe hose before proceeding.

Before ever attempting to fill your water containers, make sure that they are cleaned properly. Use 1 teaspoon of bleach plus one quarter of water in each container. Wait 30 seconds and then dump the water out. Your container will now be clean and ready for use. It is very important to add that you should never use a water container that has previously had toxic chemicals in it. Find another container.

Another rule of thumb for water storage is that it should be replaced every six months. Be sure to add dates to all of your containers and rotate them out as needed. Replace the ones that are expired. If you wish to keep your water for longer than six months, water-preserving agents are available. These will give your water about a five-year shelf life. Water that is older than six months can have a quality water filter applied to it to extend its life.

Also, if you have pets, be sure to store at least a half a gallon of water per day for each of your animals.

GATHERING RAIN WATER

No survival situation is predictable, and that is precisely why it is important to understand how to successfully gather and store rainwater. It should be noted that gathering rainwater is actually against the law in some states, and others it is regulated. For the purpose of this section, we are discussing gathering this water in extreme emergency situation where there are no regulations or laws due to a major global collapse or disaster. If you seek to put some of these methods and use now, please check with your local laws and ordnances beforehand.

There are several reliable methods for collecting rainwater, and they are as follows:

- **Obtain & Use Rain Barrels**. These containers can be bought at your local hardware store. You can also make one yourself. These containers are typically made of plastic and are usually position below a downspout in order to collect water that is running off of the roof of a structure. These containers typically have a small spout towards the bottom is used release water or connector garden hose. Some store-bought rain barrels even have covers that come with them for keeping out Boggs, small children and animals.

- **Use a Rainwater Catchment System**. These are massive tanks that are stored underground for the collection of rainwater from roofs and gutters. After the system collects the water, it filters it and pumps it into your home for safe use. The filtered rainwater can be used for cooking, bathing, or anything else.

- **Use a Rain Chain**. These are typically used instead of traditional downspouts. Rain chains are typically made of copper and are used to guide rain from your roof. The rain runs down the chain, which are actually small cups, ending up in your garden, rain barrel or other collection system that you have installed.

- **Use Household Items.** Other items can be used to capture rainwater as well. You can use simple watering cans, child size swimming pools and small pots to collect water for later use. It is very important to filter this water before using it for any other purpose than watering your garden. Any container that you use to collect water should be covered to keep out mosquitoes and other nuisances.

GATHERING WATER FROM OTHER NATURAL SOURCES

You can gather water from a variety of different sources. If rainwater is not an option, you can obtain water from lakes and rivers as well. There are a few things to keep in mind before you attempt this. Any water that you gather from a natural source should be purified before you ever try to drink it. This will greatly reduce the chances of you and your loved ones coming into contact with bacteria or other contaminants.

Here are a few pointers that help you one gathering your own water supply for later use:

- Examine the plants around the water source before you gather any for yourself. Do they look healthy? This will be a good indicator of whether or not you should proceed with using the water.

- Is the body of water located in or near an area that has suffered contamination in the way of chemicals for bacteriological agents? Never ever use water that might be contaminated! Not even the best purification methods are enough to ensure

100% safety with a contaminated water source. Water purification will eliminate many contaminants, but not all of them. Deadly chemicals could still remain from the source event that introduced the toxic agents, which is exactly why it should be avoided.

- Always gather your water from a running source. Seek out a section of the river or lake where there is flowing water. Do not collect water from a standard source.

- Though it has been stressed before, I will stress it again: make sure that your waters just carefully purified and stored in a clean containers for drinking. This cannot be stated enough!

SURVIVAL MEDICINE:

PLANTS

Whether you are starting an off-the-grid medicine garden, or just want to know what wild plants can be used for medical purposes when you are on the move after a disaster, this section is something that you will want to read.

Learning how to diagnose and treat wounds and illnesses when no ambulance is coming can be the difference between life and death. This book explains how to treat common ailments, what plants preppers should learn to grow (or spot in the wild) and what medicines are a good idea to stock pile.

It goes without saying that you should familiarize yourself with these plants before the stress of a disaster drops your learning curve dramatically. Taking the time to visit a garden center and see the plants in person will make identifying them in the wild easier and safer. You also do not want to discover that you have been doing something the wrong way when your family is counting on you to get it right.

NETTLE (URTICA DIOCIA)

This weedy-looking plant serves many medicinal purposes.

The leaves can be eaten raw or cooked and are similar in taste and texture to spinach. Added to a tea, it can treat acidosis.

It is also used as a pain-reliever for arthritis and chronic bladder irritation.

MARIGOLD (CALENDULA OFFICINALIS)

Despite not being high in tannins, marigolds are considered astringents. They can be used externally for minor burns, wounds and skin abrasions, as well as internally for stomach irritation. The flowers are edible and can be used as a foodstuff.

COMFREY (SYMPHYTUM OFFICINALE)

The leaves and roots can be used externally to heal cuts and other skin abrasions in compresses or ointments.

ALOE VERA

Aloe Vera is mostly commonly used as a topical gel for thermal and radiation burns. The thick leaf can be fileted open and the gel removed. However, there are countless other benefits. Its juice can be made into an electrolyte-balancing drink, and it is known to lower high cholesterol and blood pressure, as well as treat candida infections. It can also treat arthritis joint pain.

CATTAIL (TYPHA)

This plant has a LOT of uses. The roots are considered antiseptic and can be used for toothaches, wounds, burns, stings, cuts, bruises and burns. The seed heads can be used as torches, insulation, fire transportation, tinder and a wilderness pillow. Additionally, you can make arrow shafts out of the stalk. The stalks and leaves can be woven into hats, mats, baskets and shelter roofing.

HORSETAIL (EQUISETUM)

Horsetail tea is good for nasal congestion, dry cough, bronchitis, flu-and-cold fevers, and digestive regularity. Inhaling horsetail vapor may also help relieve congestion.

Horsetail foot soaks are also believed to help relieve athlete's foot and combat frostbite. Gargling with a horsetail mouthwash will also help with sore throats and swollen gums. To make the mouth waste, boil 1 teaspoon of herb per cup of water.

If you are hungry, you can eat the stalk just like you would asparagus.

BASIL (OCIMUM BASILICUM)

Basil has so many medicinal uses that I am going to have to break them down a list. Read on to learn how much this common kitchen herb can do for you when SHTF.

Fever: Basil leaves can be used to treat fevers associated with both malaria and dengue. Leaves should be tender and boiled. The leaves are germicidal and will help combat several types of bacterial and viral infections.

Cold and Cough: Chew fresh basil leaves or make a tea to calm coughs and help expectorate mucus in the bronchial tubes.

Stings and bites: Basil juice applied to a sting or bite will relieve pain and help draw poison out of the body.

Headache: Vapors from a pot of water and basil leaves is helpful in relieving headaches.

Use one tablespoon to every 2 cups water and

inhale for 5-10 minutes.

PINE TREES

If you find yourself in a situation where all you have are pine trees, you have more to work with than you may think you do. Pine needles are a much better source of vitamin C than even oranges (4-5 times better!), and their sap is an excellent for externally treating sores and burns.

To make pine needle tea, take a handful of clean pine needles and place them in a cup. Pour boiling water into the cup and let the needles steep. It is ready when the needles have paled.

The Native Indian Costanoan people also chewed on pine sap to treat rheumatoid arthritis.

MINT (MENTHA)

Mint is an excellent source of vitamins A, C and B2. It is a powerful antioxidant and can help relieve nasal and chest congestion as well as mild cramps. It is evenly being studied for its potentially cancer-preventing capabilities.

When steeping mint into a tea, the most vital step is to cover the cup or pot while steeping.

CINNAMON

Cinnamon can be made into a tea to ease menstrual discomfort and migraines. Ground cinnamon can be blended with raw honey to make natural cough syrup.

When storing cinnamon, make sure that it is authentic cinnamon and not cassia cinnamon. Cassia is what is commonly sold in grocery stores and lacks any of cinnamon's medicinal properties. Ground cinnamon also degrades quickly, so store yours in stick form.

BEESWAX

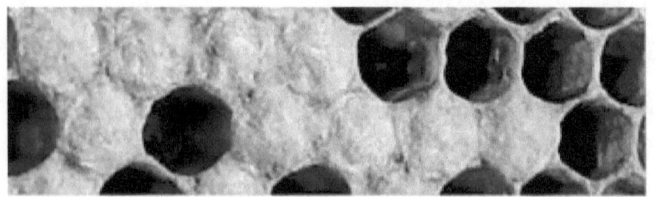

Beeswax is excellent for external healing. It is an excellent skin protectant for cold weather and can be easily combined with other natural herbs to make soothing balms.

For Rashes and Itching: Melt 1/4 cup's worth of beeswax and combine with 1 tablespoon of comfrey powder, 1 tablespoon chickweed powder and apply (while cool, not hot!) to affected area.

Cracked Lips: Dehydration and bitter cold can wreak havoc on the sensitive skin on lips. If not taken care of, they can crack and bleed. Soften a small bit of beeswax by rubbing it between your fingers and applying it to your lips.

If you have the resources and the time, you can melt down 2/3 cups of beeswax and combine it with 1 tablespoon of honey and a few drops of peppermint oil to make a boutique lip balm.

HOT PEPPERS

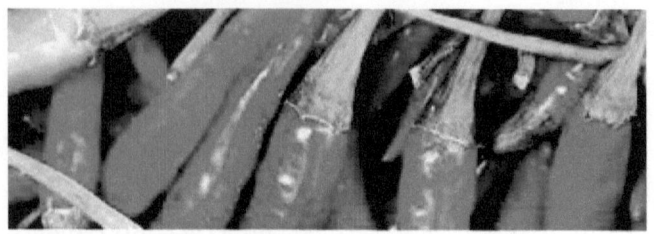

Any hot pepper can quickly become a topical anesthetic to relieve pain or be taken in a tea to relieve cold and flu congestion, as well as abdominal distress.

For congestion or gastrointestinal distress: Chop up 2 hot peppers (jalapeños, for example) per cup of water, and add honey and ginger if any is available. It will certainly open up your sinuses! Capsaicin has antifungal properties, which will help fight off sinusitis.

Capsaicin interacts with Substance P, which is involved with the inflammatory process. In a pinch, a topical application could help with nerve pain, arthritis and neuropathy.

SURVIVAL MEDICINE:

PROCEDURES

TREATING BURNS

Even when ambulances are available and help is on the way, treating a burn immediately is extremely important. The destruction of tissue will continue further down into the skin the longer that it is untreated.

No matter what degree the burn is, there are three goals that you have to keep in mind:

1. Prevent shock.

2. Prevent risk of infection.

3. Ease pain.

There are also some things that you need to remember NEVER to do, no matter how tempting:

1. Do not pop blisters.

2. Do not peel dead skin.

3. Do not peel cloth off of the skin.

4. Do NOT apply butter. This popular folk remedy will attract bugs and create a nightmare.

FIRST DEGREE BURN

How to Visually Diagnose:

The skin will be red. However, there is no broken skin and no blisters are present. Some inflammation is normal.

How to Treat:

Running the affected area under cool water and apply a burn cream or natural remedy such as aloe vera.

SECOND DEGREE BURN

This is most likely the burn incurred from coming in contact with hot water or a quick kerosene burn. It is more serious than a first degree burn and bodily liquids will rush towards the surface of the skin in blisters.

How to Visually Diagnose:

The surface will be red and splotchy. Some blisters will form, and the area may weep or ooze. However, there is no broken skin.

How to Treat:

Submerge the affected area in cool water for at least five minutes. If the burns are relatively minor, you can apply a sterile cloth or bandage. It they look a little more serious, wrap a bandage in plastic (so the cloth won't stick to the burn) and cover the burn. Treat with burn cream or aloe vera when possible, but do NOT pop any blisters in the process.

THIRD DEGREE BURN

A third degree burn is a serious and potentially fatal medical emergency. Treat immediately. These can happen when coming in contact with boiling pots of water, falling in a campfire and getting electrocuted.

How to Visually Diagnose:

The skin will be quite literally burned – it will be charred white and the skin will be cracked and broken.

How to Treat:

Situation 1: If the person is in shock, you need to deal with that before you deal with the burn. Perform CPR to stabilize them.

Situation 2: If you suspect that chemicals (such as acids or bleach) were involved, and you still have access to a working phone, immediately call a Poison Control Center at 1-800-222-1222 for specific instructions on how to deal with the chemical you are dealing with.

Situation 3: When you have established that the person is not in shock, remove any jewelry and clothing surrounding the affected area. The surrounding areas will swell greatly. Treat the area with cool water, but not cold water and not with ice. Using ice can push the patient into shock. Elevate the affected area above the patient's heart. If hospitals still exist, get the patient to a hospital as quickly as possible. The possibility of infection and complication is very high and the patient must be kept indoors and in a very clean environment. If they go into shock during treatment, perform CPR.

TREATING HYPOTHERMIA

Hypothermia claims over 600 people a year, even when there are no disasters and hospitals are still available. It is crucial that you understand what hypothermia does to the body, what makes it worse, and how to treat it.

Hypothermia is what happens when a body drops below the average core temperature (95-98.6 Fahrenheit / 35-37 Celsius). The temperature drop affects all of the body's organs and slows the patient's mind and body down, which makes the possibility of making a mistake and getting into an accident much higher.

Cold water is much more dangerous than cold air — about 25 times more dangerous. Generally speaking, thinner bodies and the very old or very young are more likely to die of hypothermia.

How to Diagnose:

It will usually sneak up on someone, so they will not be the best judges of whether or not they have hypothermia. Their judgment will become impaired as their brain slows down. The person's core temperature will be much lower than normal. They should be cold to the touch. If you unable to gage an approximate body temperature, look for involuntary shivering. The body will attempt to raise its temperature by shaking almost uncontrollably.

How to Treat:

Remove wet clothes from the patient and cover them in a dry blanket or other covering. Shield them from the wind, but especially their neck and head. Use warm compresses and offer warm liquids. Do NOT use hot compresses or liquids, the drastic difference could shock the body. Be gentle and avoid physical shocks. The person needs to be as inactive as possible to keep the cold from spreading from extremities to the central parts of the body too quickly.

TREATING HEAT

EXHAUSTION

Heat exhaustion is potentially fatal, if allowed to progress to heat stroke. Take steps to treat the condition immediately.

How to Diagnose:

The person will be weak, nauseated, dizzy and possibly vomiting. The body will be low on fluids and electrolytes and be too hot.

Hot to Treat:

Get the person out of the heat and indoors, if possible. Fan them and get them into a shady area. Shield them from the sun and apply cool compresses, splash them with cool water and pay particular attention to the armpits and groin. Do not administer caffeinated or alcoholic drinks. Administer cool drinks, but not cold drinks. Do not allow the person to drink too quickly, but encourage them to pace themselves to avoid vomiting. Avoid physical activity for the rest of the day. If medical facilities still exist, get the person in contact with a doctor for a follow-up, that same day if symptoms last longer than

one hour. They may have a mild headache after

suffering from heat exhaustion.

THE ALL-MIGHTY BANDANA

There are at least 51 different survival uses for a bandana. Have plenty around, as some of these uses will either consume the bandana or mark them as personal hygiene items.

MEDICAL USE

1. Finger Splint

2. Wrist Brace

3. Ankle Wrap

4. Sling

5. Splint Tie

6. Cold Pack

7. Hot Pack

8. Tourniquet

9. Compress

10. Washcloth

11. Poultice

12. Pressure-bandage tie

DRINKING WATER USE

13. Reusable Tea Bag

14. Sediment Strainer

15. Dew Collector

16. Sponge

17. Wick clarifier

RESCUE USE

18. Trail Marker

19. Signal Flag

20. Ground Signal Panel

PROTECTIVE USE

21. Sun Protector

22. Dust Mask

23. Earmuffs

24. Headband

25. Hand Wrap

26. Makeshift Socks

27. Hat

28. Scarf

29. Belt

30. Facemask

31. Shoelaces

32. Sunglasses / Light Filter

TOOL USE

33. Fire Windscreen

34. Fire Starter

35. Cordage

36. Sling – Weapon

37. Food Wrap

38. Flashlight Cover

39. Plate

40. Bear Bag

41. Lamp Wick

42. Stuff Sack

43. Lashing

44. Pack

45. Net

46. Pot Holder

47. Bug Cover

HYGIENE USE

48. Toothbrush / Oral Hygiene

49. Towel

50. Toilet Paper

51. Feminine Hygiene

EDIBLE BUGS

While many people don't even like the thought of a bug within a few feet of where they're standing, they can actually be the difference between living and dying when the "stuff" hits the fan. Indeed, lots of bugs are actually edible—and some of them are delicious! In extreme cases of survival, it is good to know exactly which bugs can be eaten and which ones you should avoid at all costs. There are several pointers to keep in mind when scavenging for bugs in the woods:

1. Don't eat brightly colored bugs. Stay away from them. In nature, bright colors are usually indicators of danger. To be safe, it's better to look for other sources of food.

2. Do not eat bugs that are already dead.

3. Avoid eating bugs that give off a foul odor. The only exception is the stinkbug.

4. Never attempt to catch and eat a bug that is capable of biting or stinging. Some of them are edible (Bees), but you should have plenty more opportunities to obtain a meal, so there's no point in getting hurt. Besides, you might have an allergy that you didn't know about, and the sting could set it off.

5. Avoid bugs that are known to carry diseases. This includes mosquitos, ticks, and flies.

6. Stay away from poisonous insects. This includes spiders and scorpions. Some suggest that it's okay to try after they have been properly killed and cooked, but I do not suggest this. It's simply not worth the risk.

Now that we understand what not to eat, let's have a look at what we can eat. The list below explains which bugs can be caught, prepared, and eaten. I also explain how to prepare them in cases where special conditions must be met.

EDIBLE BUG LIST

- **Ants**: Leafcutter Ants, Honeypot Ants and Lemon Ants

- **Agave Worms**: These worms are significant source of protein.

- **Bees**: These can be prepared however you like. Fry them, bake them, roast them, or just add them to your cook pot. They taste somewhat like bacon and mushrooms when cooked.

- **Bamboo Worms**: These worms are predominantly found in Thailand. They're considered a healthier option than most meats and are delicious when fried.

- **Beetles**: It's thought that more than 30 percent of the world's population enjoys eating the occasional beetle. They are typically eaten fried.

- **Centipedes**: They have a very crunchy texture and a somewhat savory flavor. It's important to be careful when catching them; they can bite you and cause swelling.

- **Caterpillars**: These bugs can be boiled, fried, or dried out.

- **Cicadas**: While they look unappealing at first, cicadas are actually a tender and juicy dish.

They can be cooked or eaten raw, but cooking them does eliminate the possibility of ingesting nasty bacteria.

- **Cockroaches**: These bugs are extremely healthy, and it has been said that they taste like chicken. They should be cooked thoroughly at a high temperature before eating.

- **Crickets**: Crickets are rather popular in dishes in Mexico and Thailand. They can be prepared in a variety of ways. Your imagination is the limit.

- **Dragonflies**: These bugs are best fried or boiled.

- **Earthworms**: These creatures are high in iron and protein. They can be cooked or eaten raw.

- **Grasshoppers**: These bugs are quite high in calcium and protein.

- **Hornworms**: They have a flavor somewhat reminiscent of green tomatoes and shrimp. Cook thoroughly before eating.

- **Stinkbugs**: They are extremely high in vitamin B and even have minor analgesic properties. Let them soak overnight in a container of water before cooking to remove their signature odor before eating. Also, they have been known to survive being cooked, so be sure to cook them thoroughly to be on the safe side.

- **June Bugs**: High in nutrients. They can be roasted over hot coals for a crunchy snack. Native Americans used to eat them frequently.

- **Leeches**: If there is a body of water nearby, chances are good that leeches are there in large numbers. They are normally ground down into a paste and cooked before eating.

- **Mealworms**: They can be served in a number of ways and taste somewhat like shrimp.

- **Wasps**: Don't get stung! It might be best to avoid this bug, but if you decide to catch some, they can be prepared however you want. They are best served with rice if you have some handy.

- **Waxworms**: Also known as wax moth larvae. Cook well before eating. They have a flavor similar to pine nuts.

- **Walking Sticks**: They have a somewhat leafy flavor and can be cooked using whatever methods are available to you at the time.

There are many other bugs that can be eaten, and the good news is that most of them are packed with essential nutrients. In fact, edible bugs are far better for us than most meat products. Just make sure to be careful; don't try to eat something you're not sure about. You don't want to make a mistake and risk your health. Always stick with the bugs you know and be sure to cook them

thoroughly to avoid contact with germs.